YOU MUST FORGET!

A Soul's Journey of Choosing,
Forgetting, and Becoming

Teetee Cubes

DEDICATION

To my parents, thank you for giving me life and the roots that shaped me.

To my siblings, for walking this journey beside me in your own way.

To my chosen circle — Tolu, Mochi, Temi, Bukola, Winnie — your friendship holds me together in more ways than you know.

To my entire family — blood and beyond — thank you for being part of the story.

And to you, the reader — may these words plant a seed in your spirit,
and may you find peace on the journey you chose... although you had to forget.

With all my love,
Teetee Cubes

"Akúnlẹ̀ yàn l'adáyé bá, adé ayé tan ojú nkan wá." - A yoruba adage

We chose our path in stillness,
before breath, before form.
We bowed to a journey unknown,
drawn by purpose, not comfort.

But Earth crowned us with names and noise,
and we forgot what we once knew.
We chased what only eyes could see -
yet the soul... still remembers.

CONTENTS

♦ ♦ ♦

There is a place that exists outside of time.
No clocks, no death, no hunger. Only energy, memory, and choice.

Here, souls do not walk, they drift. Some glow with experience, others shimmer like stars, new and curious. All of them come here for the same reason: to choose.

The room stretches endlessly, filled with shelves that spiral into the ether. On each shelf, a life! Tucked inside, like a memory waiting to be lived. Each one is a collectible — packaged with emotion, growth, joy, and suffering. No life is perfect. But every life is precious.

Today, one soul hovers near a display. Not the most glamorous life. Not the easiest. But it calls to her. Gently at first, then with force. She senses what this life contains: Heartbreak and Healing. Loneliness and legacy. A story of resilience and reinvention. Of remembering who she is — and choosing to forget.

A Guide appears beside her — not a teacher, but a companion. Soft, ageless, watching.

"You've seen the preview."
"Yes," she says.
"You understand what this life will cost?"

  I do."
"Then it's time."
"What if I forget why I chose it?"
"You will."
"And what if I never remember?"
The Guide smiles.

"That is the point."

She places her hand over the life. It flickers, then dissolves into her essence. The Guide speaks one final time.

"YOU MUST FORGET."

And with that, she falls. Fast and silent — toward time, toward matter, toward Earth.

1. AKÚNLẸ̀ YÀN

There's a belief, deeply rooted in the wisdom of the Yoruba people of Nigeria, that before we are born, each soul makes a conscious choice. In quiet agreement with the Creator, we select our life. The family we will be born into, the body we will inhabit, the joys we will experience, and even the challenges we must face. It's not random. It's not punishment. It's purpose.

No one forces your hand.

No one pushes your soul. You lean into the life you're meant to live, drawn by something only you can feel. A hunger. A lesson. A vibration.

Let's explore that for a moment....

Not as doctrine, not as fact, but as a possibility.

What if you're not here by accident?

What if your life has a purpose deeper than you can see?

What if the Creator knew you fully and intentionally, even before your first breath?

What if you chose this path... and then had to forget, so you could truly live it?

What if...

... you chose your family?

... you chose the success?

... you chose the lessons?

… you chose the failure?

Maybe you didn't just appear. Maybe you were sent — by a Creator who knows you deeply. What if your life wasn't random? What if you were known long before your first breath, and set apart for something only you could carry?

Now, pause and reflect…

If you remembered it was all a story, would you still cry?

If you knew you couldn't fail, would you still try?

If you knew every loss was love in disguise, would you still grieve?

"I knew you before I formed you in your mother's womb. Before you were born…" —*Jeremiah 1:5 (NLT)*

2 THE EARLY ECHOES

No one arrives here as a blank slate. From the moment we enter the world — wide-eyed, vulnerable, full of wonder — we begin walking through the echoes of the life we once chose, even when we don't remember choosing it.

Childhood shapes us in ways we're still discovering. Some were born into warmth and security. Others had to fight to be seen. Maybe your earliest memory is filled with laughter, or maybe it's the sound of a slammed door. Either way, it left a mark.

I carry some of those early marks too.

When I was nine, I had to attend school in a different state, away from my parents — which meant I had to live with relatives, who didn't treat me well. Somewhere deep inside, a quiet seed of abandonment began to grow. I wondered where my parents were in all of it. I felt misplaced, unsure, even abandoned. I was young — far too young to explain what I needed, but just old enough to know something wasn't right. I didn't have words for the ache, so I studied hard instead. That was how I survived. That's how I found some kind of light.

Somehow, I kept rising. I did well in school, even representing my state at national competitions. Although I had to fight through a lot, something kept me going. I didn't know it then, but God was quietly there — steady in the background, guiding me in ways I couldn't yet recognize. His presence was always with me, even when I didn't have the words for it.

**This chapter isn't just about me.
It's about you, too.**

What shaped your childhood?
Not just the events — but the emotions beneath them.
Did you feel chosen? Protected? Invisible? Did you have to grow up too soon?
Were you told who you were, or did you have to figure it out on your own?

Sometimes, it takes years to see the patterns. Sometimes, we don't realize we're still living from that younger version of ourselves — still proving, still protecting, still pretending.

What if the child you once were had a deeper purpose? What if the version of you that struggled was never behind… just becoming? And what if — even in the moments that felt chaotic, unfair, or lonely —you were still walking the story your soul once said 'yes' to?

Like Joseph, you may find yourself in places you didn't deserve. A pit. A prison. A season that feels unfair. But even there, **God is with you** — just as HE was with Joseph when the world forgot him. HE was with Daniel in the lion's den. HE stood in the fire with Shadrach, Meshach, and Abednego — not outside it, but in it.

And HE is with you, right now

Whether you are rising or rebuilding,

thriving or just holding on.

In clarity and in confusion,

in joy, in quiet, in longing.

Even now, as you read these words — HE is here!

"And be sure of this: I am with you always, even to the end of the age."

— Matthew 28:20 (NLT)

3 THE SILENT TEACHER

Maybe your soul knew exactly what it was signing up for, before arriving earth. Maybe it chose this path, this body, this timeline — not because it would be easy, but because it would shape something eternal in you. There was clarity then. Peace. But coming into this realm required one thing: Forgetting.

And so you came. Not as a finished product, not as someone with all the answers — but as a human being, learning everything again from scratch. Like many of us, you may have reached a point in life where everything felt like it was coming undone.

I know that place. I've been there.

There was a season in my life where I felt like I was falling apart from the inside out. Outwardly, I was functioning — doing what needed to be done, staying afloat — but inside, I was barely holding on. I was in pain. I was overwhelmed. I prayed for relief, for clarity, for rescue… and all I got was silence.

At first, I thought I had done something wrong. That maybe I had drifted too far. That maybe God had quietly stepped away. It's strange how silence can feel so personal, like absence. But in time, I began to understand that silence doesn't always mean abandonment.

Sometimes, silence is sacred.
I remember the story of Shadrach, Meshach, and Abednego — three men in the Bible who were thrown into a fiery furnace. Not

because they failed, but because they refused to bow to anything less than God. If you've never read it before, you can find it in the *book of Daniel, chapter 3*. It's the kind of story that stays with you. God could have stopped it. He could have softened the king's heart or changed the outcome entirely. But He didn't. He let them go into the fire. And then — something miraculous happened. When the king looked into the flames, expecting to see them consumed, he was shocked. He turned to his advisors and asked, "Didn't we throw three men in there?" Because now he saw four. The fourth looked different — divine.

The king immediately commanded that the three men be brought out of the fire. Even the king, powerful and proud as he was, stood in awe. The fire didn't destroy them. It revealed who was with them all along.

"When you walk through the fire, you will not be burned; the flames will not set you ablaze." - Isaiah 43:2

This is not just a verse — it's a truth I've lived.

Sometimes God doesn't take us out of the fire... because He plans to meet us inside it. Maybe the pain in your life isn't meant to break you, but to show you that it can't. Maybe God has been in your fire all along, quietly holding you through the part of the story you do not understand.

Have there been seasons in your life when God felt silent?
What did you believe about yourself during those moments?
Looking back now, can you see evidence that you were being carried —
even when you felt alone?
What did silence teach you that words never could?

This realm — this life — often distracts the soul from its essence. We're pushed to achieve, to perform, to prove. And in the process, we forget who we are and who is walking with us.

HE is with you.

Even now.

Still.

Always.

"Even if a mother could forget, I will not forget you. I have written your name on the palms of my hands." — *Isaiah 49:15–16*

4 THE SOUL'S TIMELINE

We talk a lot about growth. We want to succeed, get stronger, go further. But not all growth is visible. Not all of it comes with applause. There's the kind of growth the world sees — and then there's the kind your soul was sent here for.

The verse above isn't just about material success or physical health. It's about alignment — prospering in all areas , just as your soul prospers. That part is often overlooked, but it matters more than we think.

For your soul to prosper, it must grow. And soul growth is often quiet, lonely, and confusing.

There was a time in my life when I looked like I was holding it all together — and maybe I was, depending on who you asked. Inside, I was tired. I had stepped into roles I didn't ask for. I was carrying weight I never expected.I did what needed to be done. I kept going. That's all I could do. But strength that isn't anchored in the soul will always lead to depletion.

Somewhere beneath it all, something in me began to break open — not from weakness, but from the pressure of a life that wasn't being lived from the inside out.

Then ,I remembered *Joseph* in the Bible:

He had a dream — bold, beautiful, divine.

He saw people bowing before him, a sign of favor, of purpose.

The next thing he knew, he was in a pit.

Sold. Rejected. Misunderstood.

Not because the dream was wrong…

but because the dream had to pass through development.

Because Joseph, too, had a soul — and that soul had to grow.

The crown doesn't come before the crushing.

The assignment doesn't come fully formed.

Even divine dreams require soul maturity.

Lets Pause. And reflect ….

There's a moment that will come for all of us.

A moment after all the striving, the doing, the performing. After the titles and achievements and noise. When the room grows quiet. When the world no longer needs you to prove anything.

In that moment, it will just be you… and your soul. The question won't be how far you went, or how many people clapped. The question will be whether your soul came with you.

You'll meet the version of yourself that remembers — the one that knew who you were before the world told you who to become. And maybe, just maybe... you'll hear the question that was once asked:

"What will it profit a man if he gains the whole world, yet loses his soul?" — *Matthew 16:26 (NKJV)*

Will it have been worth it?

All the late nights?

The pressure to show up a certain way?

The silent shrinking of your true self?

We grow older — but do we grow deeper?

We chase success — but do we check in with the soul that was sent here to carry it?

And here's what no one tells you:

When this life ends — your soul will remember.

It will remember what it came here to do.

It will remember who you really are.

And in that moment of truth — when the layers fall off, when it's just you and eternity — you may wish you had paid attention sooner.

So if something in you feels restless now, don't rush past it. You don't have to figure it all out in this moment.

You don't even have to stop reading or put the book down.

That tug isn't confusion - It's a call.

And it's not too late.

It's right on time.

You don't have to believe it yet.

Just sit with it.

Let it stir something ancient within you!

5 THE BODY REMEMBERS TOO

The soul isn't the only part of you that remembers.
The body does too.It carries the echoes of every story you've lived. The tension in your shoulders. The tightness in your chest. The way your stomach reacts when something feels off. Your body is always been speaking — even when you aren't listening.

It is the house your soul chose. The temple your journey lives in. It carries the echoes of the life you are living — the moments that felt like too much, and the seasons that never felt like enough. It holds your strength, your hesitation, your endurance. It stores the quiet stories you didn't have the words for.

Some of us know what it means to stretch — food, energy, time, faith. We know what it means to make small things last. To show up tired. To smile anyway.

Others may have lived with more certainty — more stability, more provision. But even abundance doesn't exempt us from burden. Lack doesn't always look like an empty wallet. Sometimes it looks like an overwhelmed heart.

The body remembers all.

It remembers what you endured and what you withheld.
It remembers the way your back straightened when you needed to look strong. It remembers the tears you held in, the breath you never fully exhaled.

And still, somehow… you kept going.

There's a quiet strength that forms in survival — one that often goes uncelebrated. It's not glamorous. It's not loud, but it is powerful.

Sometimes, it looks like preparing dinner with what's left in the fridge. Sometimes, it's like sending the application when you feel unqualified. Other times, it's like getting up again, even when you're afraid of what the day might hold.

This chapter is not about survival. It's about what your body has carried — and how your soul is learning to catch up. Whether you've known hardship or haven't had to worry much at all, the invitation is the same:

Pay attention to your body.

Has it been running on fear?

On pressure?

On expectations that never let up?

Have you rewarded it only when it performs?

Or punished it when it asks for rest?

The body is not your enemy.

It's not just flesh. It's not a costume.

It's the partner your soul chose to carry you through this life.

So pause, even now.

Place your hand on your chest. Feel the rhythm.

That's not just breath — that's testimony.

You are here.

Not just because your soul is strong —but because your body has carried you through things you never thought you'd survive.

Let it rest.

Let it breathe.

Let it heal.

Because the body remembers too.

And it has waited long enough for you to notice.

6 LOVE, AND THE LESSON

Somewhere along the soul's journey, certain people appear — not by accident, but by design. They show up as friends, lovers, partners, even strangers who feel strangely familiar. I believe we meet them because our souls once agreed to. Maybe, before we arrived here, we made soul contracts — quiet promises to cross paths, to stretch one another, to teach the lessons we couldn't learn alone. I call them soul allies. Not all of them stay forever. Some love us deeply. Some break our hearts, but all of them shape us.

Love, especially, becomes one of the most powerful classrooms. It isn't a detour from the journey — it is the journey. It stretches us. It mirrors us. It reveals both our brightest and our most broken parts. And when the story has taught what it came to teach, we don't always need to hold on with pain or bitterness. Letting go, too, can be an act of grace. Because sometimes the real assignment was never to keep them... but to find ourselves again after they leave.

I know this not just in theory — I've lived it.

I got married to my forever love — or so I thought. We had vows, dreams, and plans. We built a life together, or at least the outline of one. There were genuine moments of joy. Real love. Laughter that lives somewhere in my memory, even now. I remember holding onto the hope of expanding our love through a child. I prayed with my whole heart for that. But while I was praying, he was giving that miracle to someone else.

The pain was sharp, but quiet. Not loud or dramatic — just crushing in a way that left me breathless. And somehow, even before the truth fully unraveled, I knew. I knew it was done. The home we built stopped being a place where truth could live. Outside forces interfered. Choices were made that I could not unfeel. Things began to fracture — slowly at first, then all at once. And eventually, the marriage ended.

This is not a chapter of blame.

It's a chapter of becoming. Because when the marriage ended, something else quietly began — the long walk back to myself. Love had shown me beauty, yes. But it had also shown me how far I had wandered from the girl I once was. In loving deeply, I had forgotten parts of myself. I had put "us" before "me" so many times that I didn't recognize what was left.

Still, I don't regret the love. Even though it ended. Love taught me so much. It showed me what it meant to share life with someone, and what it means to lose that connection. It taught me how deeply I could feel, how much I could survive, and how sacred it is to choose yourself again — not out of anger, but out of clarity. Some people think heartbreak ruins you, but I believe it reveals you. And if you let it, it will return you to the center of who you are — not bitter, but refined.

Maybe you've had your own soul allies — people who came into your life like light, or like storms. Some stayed. Some left. Some taught you through joy. Others through deep, complicated pain. I want you to know, that none of them were random.

What if the people who've shaped you most were never meant to stay forever, but to leave an imprint that would awaken something in you? What if even the ones who hurt you were part of a much larger story — a soul agreement that said, I will meet you there, and I will help you grow, even if it breaks us both a little?

It's not always easy to believe that, but with distance, we begin to see things differently. And with compassion, we begin to heal.

Because when you see others as fellow travelers — each with their own path, their own forgetting, their own pain — you start to release the weight of resentment. You stop taking everything so personally. You remember: they're not just characters in your story. You're in theirs too.

So be kind.

To the ones who stayed. To the ones who left.

To yourself, most of all!

7 GOD

"So do not fear, for I am with you; do not be dismayed, for I am your God."
- Isaiah 41:10 (NIV)

There's a moment in the book of Job that has always stayed with me. After everything was taken from him — his children, his wealth, his health — Job asked the kind of questions most people are too afraid to ask. He didn't sugarcoat his grief. He asked directly: Why? Why me? Why now? Why would a good God allow such suffering?

Instead of giving simple answers, God responded with questions of His own. He asked Job, *"Where were you when I laid the foundations of the earth?"* He asked if Job could command the morning, if he could loosen the cords of Orion. God didn't dismiss Job's pain — He expanded Job's perspective. He reminded him that there is more happening than what we can see. That we are held inside a story far bigger than our suffering. And yet, still, God was there. Aware. Responding. Not ignoring him — engaging him.

That part always struck me. That the God of the universe didn't offer a neat explanation — He offered presence, awe, and a reminder of just how intimately involved He's always been.

I believe I knew that God before I came here.

Before I took on a name, a body, a timeline, I believe I sat with HIM

— in a realm beyond memory. I can't prove it, but I've felt it in the deepest parts of me. There, I believe He showed me glimpses of what this life would hold. Not as punishment, but as purpose. And HE didn't just show me — HE stayed with me.

That's why, in my most painful seasons — when love fell apart, when I didn't know who I was anymore, when silence became louder than any prayer — I didn't feel entirely abandoned. Something in me still remembered. Not everything. Just enough to sense that I was not alone.

There were times I didn't pray, not because I stopped believing, but because I didn't know what to say. But even then, I knew HE was there. I didn't feel watched in a judging way — I felt understood. Seen. Still held.

God didn't step back when things got messy. He didn't flinch when I was angry, or confused, or heartbroken. He didn't need me to get it all right. HE stayed. With full awareness of the weight I was carrying.
Now, when I look back, I see traces of HIM everywhere — in the quiet mercy that softened hard moments, in the strength that showed up unexpectedly, in the endings that eventually made space for something new. HE was never far. I just couldn't always feel Him in real time.

Maybe you've wondered where God was in your story. Maybe you still do. Maybe someone gave you a version of God that felt conditional, silent, or removed. And maybe you've been carrying that version ever since. I want to offer you the God I've come to know. The God who doesn't leave when others do. The God who doesn't require a perfect life to draw near. The God who can handle your doubts, your disappointments, and your deepest questions — and still remain.

HE is not only present in the polished parts of your life. HE is there in the confusion. In the middle of the night. In the moments when you question your own worth. HE is there when you're strong and when you're falling apart. HE sees all of it — and HE stays.

If you feel distant from HIM now, just know: HE's not distant from you. You don't have to climb back into favor or clean up the mess first. HE already knows. HE already understands. HE's the One who has been with you since before the beginning — and HE's still with you now.
HE is the One who never left.

HE listens to the parts we hide from everyone else.
HE speaks gently when shame shouts too loud.
HE holds space for both our praise and questions.

"You are not alone," HE reminds us. *"You never were."*

8 THE REMEMBERING

There comes a time in the soul's journey when remembering begins. It doesn't always happen suddenly or dramatically. More often, it arrives as a quiet shift — a subtle awareness that something within you is waking up. You begin to notice patterns, question old assumptions, and feel drawn to something deeper. It doesn't always make sense at first, but it resonates. There's a knowing, a familiarity you can't quite name.

I believe we chose this life — not every detail, but the shape of it. I believe we entered into soul contracts, sacred agreements made before birth. We chose the families we would be born into, the lessons we would face, the people we would love, and even some of the pain we would encounter. Not because we wanted to suffer, but because we knew the soul learns through contrast. We wanted to grow. We came to remember who we are.

In order to remember, we had to forget. That was part of the plan too. Forgetting allowed us to feel the full experience of being human — the doubt, the wonder, the heartbreak, the joy. The soul forgets, so that it can return to remembering with depth and humility. If we arrived already knowing, we wouldn't be able to fully feel it. But the soul does not forget forever. It only waits for the right time to awaken again.

For me, the remembering began in pieces. It came through questions. *Why this path? Why that loss? Why was I drawn to certain people, places, or dreams, without fully understanding why?* Slowly, those questions revealed something deeper — a pattern, a thread, a story that was always there. I began to see that many of the painful moments in my life had a purpose. Not one I would have chosen consciously, but one that shaped me.

I saw how the things I thought were breaking me were actually placing me back on my path. I started to feel more like myself — not the version of me shaped by fear or expectation, but the one I came here to be.

Remembering doesn't mean everything becomes easy. It means you begin to live more intentionally. You start listening to your inner voice, trusting your intuition, paying attention to the wisdom in your body and the pull of your spirit. You stop living on autopilot. You start to question who you've been performing for. You let go of the masks and move toward something realer, and deeper.

Maybe that is where you are now.

Maybe something in you has started to stir. You might not be able to explain it, but it feels like a shift — like something inside you is waking up and calling you home. That, too, is remembering. It's the soul rising above the noise and asking to be seen again.

You don't need to have it all figured out. You don't need to rush to some perfect version of yourself.

This is not a race. This is a return.

Remembering happens in how you move through the world, how you speak to yourself, how you respond to challenge, how you choose peace when you could choose performance. The more you live in alignment with who you really are, the more you remember.

Maybe this chapter is your reminder.

Maybe you've already started remembering, even without realizing it. That gentle inner shift, the quiet longing for something more — that's not confusion. **That's your soul waking up.**

You are not lost.
You are returning.
To the knowing beneath the noise,
To the voice you silenced to survive,
To the path you once chose in light
and agreed to walk in shadow.
You have not missed it.
You are not behind.
You are remembering.
Exactly on time.
And that is a sacred thing.

9 THE SOUL IN MOTION

After remembering comes movement.

Not the kind that draws attention or announces itself loudly, but the kind that begins deep within — the quiet shift, the subtle clarity, the return to something ancient and true. It's not about suddenly knowing everything. It's about beginning to feel everything differently.

You move differently when your soul is awake.

You stop asking for permission to be who you are. You stop explaining your intuition. You stop waiting to be picked. The movement isn't always physical — sometimes it's simply the decision to pause instead of perform. To choose peace instead of urgency. To follow the nudge instead of the noise.

This is what it means to live as a soul in motion.

It's not always easy. It means letting go of what made sense before. You begin to release outdated versions of yourself — identities that were built on fear, survival, or other people's expectations. You might still look the same, but everything inside you has shifted. Your silence feels different now. So does your confidence. You're no longer proving. You're no longer pretending. You're just moving — with the soul in charge.

You begin to realize you're living between realms. One foot in this world, the other in something unseen — a knowing that goes beyond logic, beyond explanation. You can still function. You go to work. You meet deadlines. You smile and play your roles. But you're also deeply aware that this life is not all there is. You sense things. You hear things in the silence. You notice when something resonates with your soul and when it doesn't.

You might not be able to explain it, but you feel it. The pull. The resistance. The alignment.

You're becoming more sensitive to the energy in a room, the tone in someone's voice, the words left unspoken. You begin to trust your gut — not as a backup plan, but as your first language. This is what happens when you live between realms.

It's not strange. It's sacred.

And from that place, your life starts to reorient. Not because you suddenly have all the answers, but because you've stopped ignoring the ones already inside you.

Soul-led living isn't about being perfect. It's about being present — tuned in to what your soul is trying to show you moment by moment. You stop outsourcing your decisions to fear or tradition. You stop betraying your peace to keep other people comfortable. You learn to pause, to ask, to feel, and then to move.

It may confuse people. It may even confuse you at times, but you'll know you're on the right path because even when it feels unfamiliar, it will feel like home.

And with that shift, something else rises — something quieter, but stronger.

A different kind of power.

Not the power that pushes. Not the kind that demands attention or dominance. But the kind that comes from deep inner alignment. The kind that whispers instead of shouts. The kind that stands in truth without needing applause.

Soft power.

It's when you know who you are — without the armor.
When you can be gentle and still be grounded.
When you don't need to control, because you trust the current.

Soft power is not passive. It's intentional. It is the calm certainty that you no longer need to convince anyone of anything. You simply show up — as you are — and that is enough. And when your soul leads, that is the kind of power you walk in.

Not to impress.
Not to dominate.
But to live fully.

Because the truth is, your presence carries weight — not because you speak the loudest, but because you are aligned. That alignment begins when the soul is allowed to move freely, without fear, without shame, without needing to forget itself anymore.

This is not the whole story.

Because we are not only soul.

We are also spirit.

That part of us that is breathed directly from God — light-filled, eternal, indestructible. It holds a different kind of knowing. A deeper kind of connection.

We will explore that when the time is right.

For now, stay here — with the soul.
Let it finish what it started.
Let it move. Let it lead.
Let it become what it came here to be.

You are remembering.

And that is enough!

So much of this journey has been about remembering — reclaiming what was forgotten, realigning with who we truly are. We've walked through what it means to live with soul. To move with intention. To lead with softness. To feel both the weight and the wonder of waking up.

But what happens if you never forgot?

*What if someone entered this life already knowing —
aware of who they were, where they came from, and why they came?*

Well… someone did.

**And in the next and final chapter of this book, we will explore who —
and what happened next.**

10 THE ONE WHO REMEMBERED

If we carried the full weight of what was coming, it could crush us before we even began. If the story we chose was beautiful, we might mistake it for something we earned, taking credit for what was grace. And if the story held pain, we might turn away from it too soon. Forgetting protects us. It allows the soul to fully enter this life — not with the burden of knowing, but with the gift of discovery.

Forgetting isn't failure. It's mercy. A sacred veil drawn for our own good, lifted only when we're ready to see.

But not everyone forgot.

There was One who remembered.

He knew the plan. He knew the cost. And still — He came.

JESUS THE CHRIST.

The Divine made flesh. God among us.

He did not forget who He was, or why He came. From the very beginning, He held full awareness of His purpose and His path. There was no veil between Him and what lay ahead. Still, He entered this world — not in pride, but in surrender.

At the wedding in Cana, when asked to perform His first miracle, *He paused.* Not because He was unsure of His power, but because He understood what that moment would initiate. Once He stepped into visibility, there was no turning back. *That wasn't just water becoming wine — it was obedience beginning to unfold.* He wasn't just performing miracles. He was walking toward sacrifice.

He remembered it all — the betrayal, the trial, the lashes, the mocking, the thorns, the weight of the cross. He remembered the pain before He ever felt it in His body. And still... He surrendered.

"Jesus, knowing all that was going to happen to him, stepped forward..."

—John 18:4 (NLT)

In the garden, He wept. Not because He was weak, but because He knew. His anguish wasn't a reaction to surprise — it was the grief of someone who remembered every detail in advance and still agreed to walk through it.His sweat looked like blood — not from wounds, but from the weight of what He remembered.

"Being in anguish, he prayed more earnestly, and his sweat was like drops of blood falling to the ground..." — Luke 22:44 (NLT)

He wasn't just preparing for suffering. He was already carrying it. Yet, unlike us, Jesus never questioned His origin or His direction. He said:

"I know where I came from and where I am going." —John 8:14 (NLT)

There was no confusion. He remembered the mission. He remembered the love that sent Him. He remembered us.

Still... He said yes.

He walked directly into everything we would run from — not because He had to, but because He chose to. He bore what we couldn't carry, so that we could live what we were meant to experience.

So if your journey feels too heavy, or if your life feels too easy and you're not sure why, if you're overwhelmed with questions about what this all means — remember this:

You were designed to forget.

You don't have to remember everything to live deeply. But you do need to remember Him. The one, whose remembrance rescued you.

The One who could not forget, — and still came.

The One who did not run from pain, but walked straight into it.

Because He remembered, we are free to live this life fully — not knowing everything, not always understanding, but trusting that the path is already held. His memory made space for our forgetting. His obedience made room for our detours. His suffering held the weight of what we couldn't carry. And still, He walked it.

There is mystery here.

Not everything needs to be explained to be true. Sometimes, it is enough to sense the thread running through your story — and know it is not random. There is a plan, even if you forgot it. There is grace, even when you can't feel it. There is love, even in the silence.

And there is One... who remembered.

And still... chose you!

A NOTE TO YOU

Dear Reader,

Thank you for walking with me. If something in these pages stirred you, sat with you, or softened something in your spirit — then maybe it was for you.

This book isn't about having all the answers. It's about remembering just enough to keep going. *It's about wondering if maybe... just maybe... your life is more intentional than it seems.*

I didn't write this to convince you of anything. I wrote it to remind you of something you already know deep inside: that your journey has meaning. That your presence here is not random. That your soul is wiser than you think.

Whether you believe in God the way I do, or in a force, or in nothing at all — I hope you felt love in these words. I hope you felt seen.

Wherever you are in your path — I honor you. I bless you, and I wish you peace on the journey you chose...

Even though you had to forget.

With all my love,
Teetee Cubes

Made in the USA
Columbia, SC
29 April 2025

57092582R00024